PENGUIN BOOKS

THE 5-DAY COURSE IN THINKING

Edward de Bono was born in Malta and after his initial education at St Edward's College, Malta, and the Royal University of Malta, where he obtained a degree in medicine, he proceeded as a Rhodes Scholar to Christ Church, Oxford, where he gained an honours degree in psychology and physiology and then a D.Phil. in medicine. He also holds a Ph.D. from Cambridge. He has had faculty appointments at the universities of Oxford, London, Cambridge and Harvard.

Dr de Bono runs the largest curriculum programme for the direct teaching of thinking in schools. Some countries, like Venezuela, have made it compulsory in all schools, and there is a growing use in Canada, the USA, China and the USSR. Dr de Bono's instruction in thinking has also been sought by such well-known corporations as NTT (Japan), Du Pont, Ericsson, United Technologies, American Standard, Exxon and Shell. His 'Six Hats' method is now used in many corporations, such as Prudential and IBM. He has also worked for governments, including the Government of California on toxic waste problems. He may be teaching senior executives of multi-national corporations one day and nine-year-olds in a primary school the next.

Dr de Bono has been invited to address such meetings as The Institute of Institutional Investors, The Commonwealth Law Conference, The American Bar Association, The World Congress on Emergency and Disaster Medicine, The World Economic Forum (Davos) and The Society of Information Managers. In 1989 he chaired a meeting of Nobel Prize laureates in Seoul, Korea.

He is the founder and director of the Cognitive Research Trust (1969) and the Centre for the Study of Thinking, and the founder of SITO (Supranational Independent Thinking Organisation) which was set up as a sort of intellectual Red Cross to provide additional and creative thinking on problems and issues. He has also set up a Task Force on Thinking in Washington.

Dr de Bono has been invited to lecture and work in forty-five countries. He has written over thirty books and there are translations available in twenty-four languages, including Chinese, Korean, Japanese, Russian, Arabic, Hebrew, Urdu, Bahasa and all major languages. He has made two television series, 'De Bono's Course in Thinking' for the BBC and 'The Greatest Thinkers' for WDR, Germany. He runs a newsletter which is published ten times a year and is the inventor of the classic L-Game which is said to be the simplest real game ever invented. He is perhaps best known for originating the term 'lateral thinking', which now has an entry in the Oxford English Dictionary.

Other titles published by Penguin:

Atlas of Management Thinking
Children Solve Problems
Conflicts: A Better Way to Resolve Them
Edward de Bono's Masterthinker's Handbook
Future Positive
Handbook for the Positive Revolution
The Happiness Purpose
I Am Right You Are Wrong
Lateral Thinking
Lateral Thinking for Management
Letters to Thinkers
The Mechanism of Mind
Opportunities
Po: Beyond Yes and No
Practical Thinking
Six Thinking Hats
Teaching Thinking
The Use of Lateral Thinking
Wordpower

Dr Edward de Bono is world-renowned for his work in the area of creative thinking. His international seminars are invariably a sell-out. For further information please contact The McQuaig Group, 132 Rochester Ave., Toronto M4N 1P1, Canada. Tel: (416) 488-0008.

THE 5 DAY COURSE IN THINKING

Edward de Bono

PENGUIN BOOKS

PENGUIN BOOKS

Published by the Penguin Group
Penguin Books Ltd, 27 Wrights Lane, London W8 5TZ, England
Penguin Books USA Inc., 375 Hudson Street, New York, New York 10014, USA
Penguin Books Australia Ltd, Ringwood, Victoria, Australia
Penguin Books Canada Ltd, 10 Alcorn Avenue, Toronto, Ontario, Canada M4V 3B2
Penguin Books (NZ) Ltd, 182–190 Wairau Road, Auckland 10, New Zealand

Penguin Books Ltd, Registered Offices: Harmondsworth, Middlesex, England

First published in the USA by Basic Books 1967
First published in Great Britain by Allen Lane The Penguin Press 1968
Published in Pelican Books 1969
Reprinted in Penguin Books 1991
10 9 8 7 6 5 4 3

Printed in Great Britain by Butler & Tanner Ltd,
Frome and London

Most people do not bother any more about their thinking
than they do about their walking or breathing. Thinking
seems a natural enough process and one is happy with one's
competence. There is, however, much more individuality in
thinking styles and sufficient difference between individuals
to suggest that thinking may be a skill about which something can be done.

The long years of education are mostly concerned with
knowledge. Fact is piled upon fact and little if any time is
spent with the basic techniques of thinking. Skill in thinking is
treated as a by-product that ought to follow detailed attention
to specific subjects. But does it? And if it does, is not this a
very roundabout and wasteful process – like burning down
the pagoda to produce roast pork? On the whole, it must be
more important to be skilful in thinking than to be stuffed
with facts.

This book has to do with thinking. The situations are chosen to
bring out points about thinking techniques just as lighting is
chosen to show up the features of a subject being photographed.

It is rather boring just to read about thinking but there can
be a lot of fun in playing around with one's own thinking

processes. This book is not a do-this and do-that book. Based on the three points of simplicity, involvement and achievement, the book is intended to amuse the reader into developing an awareness of his own style of thinking, its strong points and its weaknesses. One reader may always get blocked at a certain point. Another reader may never make use of certain strategies. Awareness is the first step to correction and improvement in any skill.

The only effort required from the reader is that he should ask himself the question: 'Why am I having difficulty over this?'

In this book nothing is taught except what is learned and that depends on the reader. The suggestions in the text are only intended to stimulate the reader's own ideas on thinking. An awake reader will get far more from the book than a dull reader and probably more than the author has put in.

Having bought this book, you are entitled to use it as you please. There is no hurry. Like the empty space in a Chinese painting, the time in which nothing happens has its purpose.

The courses are designed in leisurely, consecutive steps, and the order of these should be maintained.

July 1967   EDWARD DE BONO

The division into three different sorts of thinking (Insight Thinking, Sequential Thinking, Strategic Thinking) is by no means a rigid one. The sections overlap to some extent and particular processes may be found under different headings. The basic processes of thinking are common to all sections but certain aspects of thinking are brought out in one section more than in another. The headings are only descriptive of this different emphasis and are not instructions on how to tackle the sections.

INSIGHT THINKING: The steps leading up to the solution are not all apparent. The solution seems to come about by virtue of a sudden jump in thinking. It is more a matter of finding the right approach than of care in pursuing an approach.

SEQUENTIAL THINKING: The solution follows a progressive sequence of steps (modification, improvement, mistakes, new ideas, etc.). The sequence need not be a logical sequence; nevertheless, the steps occur one after another.

STRATEGIC THINKING: This is concerned with the choice of the most appropriate steps out of a multitude of possible steps. The search is not for a definite solution but for a policy of behaviour that is more effective than others.

Insight problems may, of course, be solved by sequential processes just as sequential problems may be solved in an insight fashion. Both processes may be used in strategic thinking.

THE FIRST 5-DAY COURSE
IN THINKING

The Bottles: Insight Thinking

Start the course tomorrow. Until then do nothing other than
consider whether your thinking is as fluent and effective as it
might be. Consider its present excellence, but consider more
whether such excellence precludes any further development.
Expect with this course either to demonstrate such excellence
or to doubt it.

The opportunities to exercise your thinking are to be real
rather than imaginary. This is a practical course, and some
equipment must be assembled.

Four empty beer or soft-drink bottles
Four table knives (preferably with flat-sided handles, and with
rounded tips – for the sake of safety)
A drinking glass filled with water.

Thinking about something is the only way to think about
thinking, and having something to show for the thinking is the
only way to judge its worth.

The first five-day course uses the sort of problem which is
usually solved quite suddenly by a flash of inspiration – what
might be called insight thinking.

PROBLEM 1

Place three bottles upright on a table or on the floor. Position them so that each bottle forms the corner point of a triangle of equal sides. The distance between the bases of any two bottles should be slightly more than the length of a knife.

Using only the four knives, construct a platform on top of the bottles. No part of any knife may touch the ground. The platform must be strong enough to support a full glass of water.

That is the problem. You may approach it as you wish. You may attack it with logic, or you may play around with the knives until something turns up. You may wait for the solution to occur to you, or you may deliberately search for it. You may even decide that the problem has no solution.

As you work on the problem observe the ease with which you solve it. Observe how long it takes you. Observe how you set about it. Observe the different approaches that you use and consider why you use them. Observe how a particular approach is blocked or comes to an end. Observe how many solutions there are, or if, in fact, there are any. If there are no solutions, observe how long it takes you to realize this and how sure you are about your decision.

The problem is intended to be an opportunity to think about your thinking. There is no frantic demand for a solution.

If you are still unsuccessful at the end of the day, you may choose to sleep on the problem, or you may choose to find out whether there is a solution by reading the next section.

Solution to the Three-Bottle Problem

Once it has been demonstrated, the solution is so obvious that it may seem incredible that it should have required any effort or time.

First, discard one knife completely. Because no more than four knives could be used does not mean that *all* four were required or had to be used. It is a common mistake in everyday thinking to assume that things must be done in a certain way and then to proceed from that assumption. Excellent thinking is of no use if based on an incorrect assumption. Most conjuring tricks and stage magic depends on the eagerness of the audience to take things for granted and only to start questioning things too late, when the trick has already been done.

The interweaving arrangement of the knife blades to give one solution is shown on page 21. A firm triangular-shaped platform is created between the bottles and resting on their tops. In the middle of this platform a full glass of water can easily be supported.

The solution seems simple enough. To arrive at it with ease would, however, be exceptional.

Why should so simple a solution be at all elusive? Perhaps when we think that we are thinking we do no more than apply ready-made patterns of experience. Had such a pattern been appropriate to this problem, the solution would indeed have been easy.

Perhaps some apparently relevant patterns interfered with the solution more than they helped it. Perhaps there was some pattern which supposed that as the distance between any two bottles was greater than a knife's length two knives would have to be used between any two bottles. Then the two knives would have to be fastened together into one sufficiently long structure. But there was nothing with which to fasten them.

Perhaps some people laid the knives so that they pointed from each bottle towards the centre of the triangle and observed that they overlapped. Perhaps this seemed a natural thing to do. Nevertheless it would have impeded the final solution.

Perhaps others did vaguely grasp the idea of an interweaving pattern, but could not quite work it out.

Mental processes are highly personal to every individual. Habit, experience, and even temperament all exert their influences. There may be wrong approaches, mental blocks, or simply a lack of inspiration. There may be a misleading confidence or an inhibiting lack of confidence.

The final solution may come about by logical effort, by chance, or not at all. Yet no one should have any difficulty in understanding the simplicity of the solution.

All those who did not solve the problem with a speedy brilliance should derive personal lessons from a consciousness of the mental processes that actually went on. This is more worthwhile than arriving at the solution.

In trying to solve the problem some may have attempted to use logic. Logic, however, requires a direction in which to proceed. If there is no obvious direction, logic may lead in the wrong direction and delay a solution or even make it impossible.

Others may have preferred chance thinking. This requires neither direction nor commitment. It is also impossible to control. Ideas arise as one toys with the knives, placing them in one position after another. Each idea is tried and discarded as it proves useless. Even as it is discarded a new idea may evolve from the failure. This may be a wasteful and a lengthy process, but it can often lead to the right solution, especially if there is no obvious direction in which to proceed logically.

The points worth noting in the first day's experience are:
1. It is important not to take things for granted at the outset.
2. The approach to the solution may be difficult if there is no pattern provided by experience.

3. Patterns provided by experience or common sense may actually hinder solution if they are not relevant.
4. The trial-and-error procedure may be just as effective as logic.

Solution to the Three-Bottle Problem

PROBLEM 2

To discover whether it is possible to construct a platform on top of four bottles, using only the four knives. Each bottle is placed upright at the corner of a square. Each side of the square is slightly longer than a knife, so that a knife fits easily between the bases of any two adjacent bottles. All four bottles must be used, and the platform must rest equally on all four. The platform must be strong enough to support a full glass of water between the bottles. Only the four knives may be used, and no part of these may touch the ground.

The problem may seem very similar to the preceding one, yet the properties of a square are different from those of a triangle. A triangle is inherently stable and because of this stability is the basis of geodesic construction. It may not be possible to treat a square shape as one treats a triangular one, which has an odd number of sides.

As before, the problem is intended as an opportunity for watching in action the personal processes involved in thinking. With the experience of the previous problem, the technique of self-consciousness should be more effective. The purpose of such awareness may also be more apparent.

You may already have decided what methods might prove effective and what dead ends can be avoided. You may even have an idea of the logical direction in which to proceed.

For all these reasons, the problem may take less time to solve than the previous one. After all, it does seem to be a very similar problem, and experience derived from the first problem should be of immense help.

Solution to the Four-Bottle Problem

The solution is very similar to that used for the three-bottle
problem. The manner in which the knife blades interweave to
form a structure strong enough to support the glass of water
is shown on page 31.

The solution is so similar to the previous one that few could
have failed to find it easily. To have missed the solution would
be as exceptional as to have found it in the first problem.

The great importance of experience in determining the ease
with which a problem may be solved is clearly demonstrated.
Had the four-bottle problem been presented before the three-
bottle one, then the ease of solution would have been reversed.

The earlier remarks about the different properties of a triangle
and a square, though true enough in a different context, had no
relevance here. The remarks were a deliberate attempt to make
things more difficult by suggesting that experience derived
from the three-bottle problem might not be applicable.

Whenever a problem is discussed in a misleading way, its
similarity to other problems may be obscured. As a result,
patterns of experience already shown to be useful, may not be

used. The deliberate attempt to suggest that the three-bottle and four-bottle problems were very different should have been ignored. Even if you thought that there might be a difference, there would have been no harm in treating the two problems as similar until they proved to be different. Regarding the second problem as similar to the first would at least have offered a line of approach. Should this have proved wrong, a consideration of why it was inadequate might have led to a better approach.

No matter with what authority misleading suggestions are made, they should be ignored or merely noted, but not allowed to interfere with the problem-solving process. There is, however, a tendency to try to save time and effort by using such hints.

The important point about the solution of the four-bottle problem is that experience acquired from the solution of the three-bottle problem can be used. The ease with which such experience is applied and the effectiveness of the application depends on how the experience has been recorded. If the experience was recorded simply as a phenomenon, as a demonstration that the thing could be done, then the experience is much less useful than it should have been.

If, on the other hand, some general principle was abstracted from the solution to the first problem, then it would be easy to remember such a principle and to apply it. Such a general principle may or may not take into account the triangular arrangement in the first problem. A very general principle may only consider how such a structure could be arranged on any number of supports independently of their number or disposition. If such a principle had indeed been derived, the four-bottle problem would not have been a problem at all. Furthermore, the attempt to mislead by suggesting a difference between the square and triangular arrangements would have been completely ineffective.

A general principle may take the following form. Starting at any corner and proceeding around the figure: knife *A* rests on knife *B*, knife *B* on knife *C*, and knife *C* rests back on knife *A*, so completing the circle and providing each knife with support at both ends. More simply, this can be stated as: proceeding in one direction, the free end of each knife rests on its neighbour.

Such a principle can be applied directly to the four-bottle situation, which requires only one more link in the chain than does the three-bottle problem. This is why the solution to the problem should have taken only a very short time.

A vague consciousness of the interweaving principle could also lead to the correct solution, but the process would take considerably longer.

Other principles or approaches may be derived from the

solution to the first problem, thereby making the solution to the second one easier.

One particular advantage of these structural problems is that it is not possible to erect them bit by bit. The structure works as a complete whole or not at all. There can be no question of only part of it being right and the rest wrong. There is no room for gradual improvement until the solution is arrived at. From the beginning the solution is complete, and it either works or it does not. In this way a definite and discernible end product is provided for the thought processes.

It is interesting at this point to examine the effectiveness of a philosophical approach to the first problem. It is usually easy to work out such approaches once the solution is known. To actually solve the problem by using such an approach can be surprisingly difficult.

One might argue that since no one of the knives can span the gap between two bottles some form of cooperation between the knives is essential. This may take several forms. There might be a sort of mutual support in which each knife both gives and receives support from each other knife at the same time. Alternatively, one knife can be used as a fastener to join the other two into a rigid structure of sufficient length. Or else one knife can be supported by the next one and that next one by the one next to it and finally back to the first one. This is, of course, the eventual solution.

The trouble with such an approach is that in practice it does not make sense. Philosophically, the final solution actually appears suspect. How, it may be asked, can any given knife derive its support from the others when their only support is that given knife which is itself unsupported? This type of approach is more often a description of a solution that has been found than a plan of action for finding one.

As before, a personal assessment of what made the solution easy or an understanding of why it was difficult or impossible is of more value than any categorical statements. Each person should define for himself the sort of comments that were listed at the end of the last section and another set of which are listed below.

1. Recognizing the essential similarity of a problem to one which has been solved before makes the problem much easier to solve.
2. It is important not to be misled by inappropriate considerations which appear to make the problem different from ones already encountered. It does not matter how firmly or on what authority such considerations are offered.
3. A specific experience is much more valuable if some general principle is derived from it.

4. The more general such a principle, the more valuable it may be.
5. The use of patterns provided by experience is the most rapid way of solving problems.

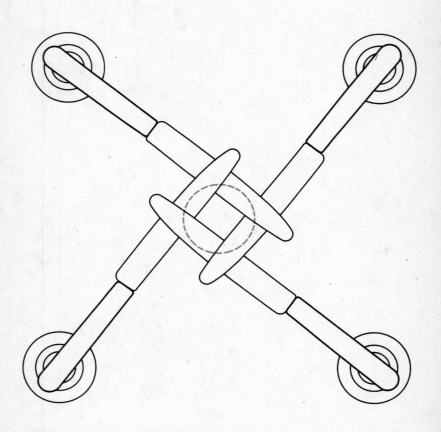

Solution to the Four-Bottle Problem

PROBLEM 3

This time use only two bottles. Place these upright, their bases separated by the length of a knife handle added to the length of a knife. The two bottles are thus farther apart than on the two previous occasions.

Using only the four knives, erect between the two bottles a bridge which will support at its centre the weight of a full glass of water. The ends of the bridge rest on the tops of the bottles. No part of any knife may touch the ground.

More important than the speed or the ease with which the problem is solved is the accuracy of description of the mental processes involved in its solution. It might even be useful to jot down notes on what appears to be happening. A note on the policy, approaches, and principles involved can provide useful insight into one's own thinking behaviour. Such disclosures may be shameful even to oneself. In the end an honest assessment of thinking habits is already a considerable improvement.

It may turn out that some one approach comes more naturally to the mind than any other. Minds have temperaments and habits even when employed in pure thinking. Once the habits are recognized, they can be deliberately encouraged if effective, or avoided if not.

To fail to solve the problem and yet to be aware of the details of that failure is more worthwhile than to solve the problem rapidly and have no idea of how it was done. This is not to imply that inspiration is valueless in that it is unlikely to have an adequate explanation. Should the solution come about by inspiration, then that is sufficient explanation. But inspiration is often set off by a chance arrangement of features, and such things can be observed.

Solution to the Two-Bottle Problem

Surprising as it may seem, there is a perfectly feasible solution
(see page 40). The structure is quite rigid and spans that
considerable gap between the bottles. It may require a little
adjusting to get the structure balanced, but this is not difficult.
If the knives do not have flat-sided handles, balancing a glass
of water in the centre of the bridge may be difficult, since it
becomes a matter of balancing a glass on a round edge. The
structure is, however, strong enough to support the full glass
of water if the handles are prevented from rolling.

The solution is based directly on the solution to the preceding
four-bottle problem. The connexion is not so obvious as that
between the three-bottle and the four-bottle problem. There is
no general principle that can be applied immediately.
Nevertheless, a careful reconsideration of the four-bottle
problem should lead to the solution.

Following the solution of this two-bottle problem is
reproduced the solution to the four-bottle problem. Regard
the knives crossing from *B* to *C* as forming a bridge between
two bottles. Consider what would happen if bottles *A* and *D*
are removed. The structure will collapse, for support of the
knife ends resting on *A* and *D* is essential to the integrity of

the structure bridging B and C. Imagine the knife supported by A extended into a long lever. Something pressing down on the other end of the lever would then replace the upward support of bottle A. The knife cannot be extended into a lever, but it can be swung completely around to occupy the position the other half of the lever would have occupied. This can be done without in any way altering the interweaving pattern. The knife is now parallel to the knife resting on D. The weight of the knife handle provides a downward force which entirely replaces the upward support provided by bottle A. The integrity of the structure is thus preserved.

The knife resting on D can be treated in a similar fashion. The bottles A and D are removed and what is left is a bridge between B and C. This is the solution to the two-bottle problem.

The solution to the four-bottle problem is thus converted into a solution for the two-bottle problem by changing the upward force provided by a supporting bottle into a downward force provided by the weight of a knife.

To derive the solution to the two-bottle problem in this way, it is necessary to be able to look at the four-bottle solution in a special way. The four-bottle solution must be regarded as a two-bottle bridge with two extra supports. The problem is then one of doing away with these supports. This involves considering a knife as part of an imaginary lever so that downward pressure on one end can be envisioned as supplying upward pressure at the other, as in a see-saw. Finally, it requires that the same knife in two separate positions be substituted for the imaginary lever.

This is indeed a complicated process. The same solution may be achieved by using only some of the above considerations. It may even be arrived at in a completely different manner.

Some may have set out to consider how the weight of the knives could be used to make a structure rigid enough to support weight. This would have constituted a new idea insofar as the mechanism had not been met in either of the two preceding problems. Such an approach may have been effective. Others may not have been able to think in so paradoxical a manner, for the basic problem seemed to be one of supporting weight. They may have been unable to consider weight as something that can be used to support weight.

By looking at weight as an asset and not just as a liability, by looking at the two-bottle problem as a four-bottle problem without two of the bottles, by looking at a support as an upward force replaceable by a downward force at the other end of a lever, by looking at a knife in two positions as forming two halves of a lever, it is possible to solve the problem.

It is a matter of looking at things not only as they are, but also as what they might be. There are usually many ways of considering something, and at times the least obvious ways prove to be the most useful. Once things have been understood as they are, it is worth looking further to see what else they might be.

At first, experience gained from the three- and four-bottle problems does not seem to be applicable to the two-bottle problem. There are no patterns that could be immediately used. A careful re-examination of the four-bottle problem is necessary before its relevance becomes apparent.

In addition to relying on general principles derived from particular experiences, it may sometimes be useful to re-examine the experiences for information which might have been overlooked if it had not seemed useful at the time.

There is a limit to the usefulness of re-examining old experiences in this way. Sometimes it is more efficient to approach the problem as a fresh one than to spend a long time seeking a parallel in past experience. It depends on how similar the other problems are, but that depends on how good one is at detecting similarities, how good at realizing that a two-bottle solution may be contained in a four-bottle one.

When there is no obvious approach to the problem and previous experience is limited, it may well be worth scrutinizing that experience in the hope of discovering some useful approach.

The
Third
Day

The following points might be noted in connexion with the two-bottle problem:

1. The ability to look at things in different ways can be very useful. It is important not to understand things only in terms of their immediate usefulness.
2. The ability to fully appreciate relationships makes it possible to manipulate them.
3. The general principles derived from experience cannot contain all the useful information of the experience, and sometimes a re-examination can be fruitful.
4. There may be different ways of arriving at the same solution.

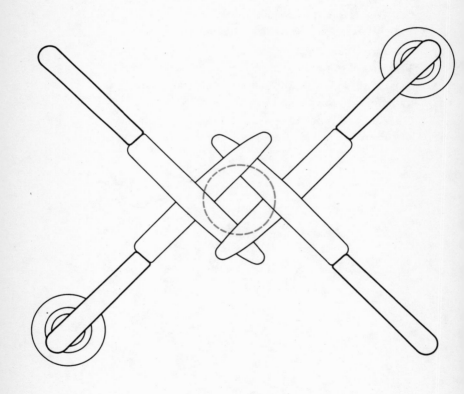

Solution to the Two-Bottle Problem

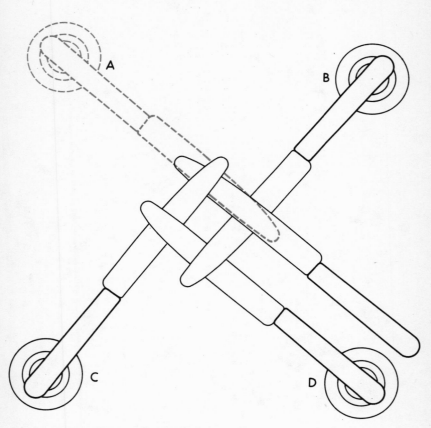

*Solution to the Two-Bottle Problem
as derived from the Four-Bottle Problem*

PROBLEM 4

Two bottles are placed upright, their bases just over a knife's length apart. Using only *three* knives, construct a bridge from the top of one bottle to the top of the other, no part of any knife is allowed to touch the ground. The bridge must be strong enough to support a full glass of water.

Either the deliberate logical processes or the haphazard trial-and-error processes may be used to solve the problem. Each person may have decided which of the two processes has proved most successful and may try to adopt that process. Others may be less certain and may prefer to use a mixture of logic and playing around as they feel inclined. Experience gained from the other problems may make the problem-solving process easier and more effective or it may be ignored.

To be effective, thinking need not be consciously controlled. The purpose of encouraging insight into thinking processes by providing a series of practical problems is not to increase control. The value of awareness lies in the recognition of mistakes and wasteful procedures. Once these have been recognized, they are likely to be avoided in the future without any deliberate effort. There is no measuring of features and careful comparisons before a face can be recognized. One encounter with a mistake may be sufficient.

Lessons are learned not by being aware that there is a lesson to be learned, but by experiencing at first hand the significance of that lesson. In addition to the notes suggested at the end of each day's section, many other personal, and perhaps better, observations should have been accumulated. Those who found the problems too easy to provide an opportunity for observing their thinking in action probably do not require such an opportunity. Such people can still amuse themselves by looking for alternative solutions and exhausting all possibilities.

Those who found the problems too difficult to solve may have gained some insight into the nature of this difficulty. A lack of imagination may not easily be remedied, but a failure to derive principles from experience or a laziness in extracting the maximum of information from experience can be altered. A habit of looking at things in different ways can be practised if too great a rigidity has been the trouble.

Each problem can be considered on its own. Each may be regarded as a practical problem for which there have been, so far, definite, correct answers. The correctness of the answer is not determined by its agreement with the solutions suggested here, but by whether the requirements of the problem have been met. In arriving at the solutions no technical knowledge or skill has been needed.

Instead of being considered separately, the problems may be taken together as a series in which experience acquired from one problem may be useful (or inhibiting) to the solution of the next. In this way the problems offer an opportunity not only for problem-solving, but, more importantly, for the handling of experience. In practical terms, the handling of experience probably occupies a larger place in our casual thinking than does pure problem-solving.

Does one passively expect experience to offer its help in solving a problem, or does one deliberately search through experience for such help? Does experience exert the same influence when it is casually come by as when it is deliberately acquired? Does the organization of experience into general principles make it easier to handle? These are questions for which there is no definite answer. Personal experience alone can provide the answers. Some minds do automatically organize experience while it is being acquired. A conscious effort to do so would only interfere. Other minds appear to derive little from experience unless an effort to organize is made.

Experience may be easily accessible to some minds, but unavailable to others unless consciously and carefully recalled. At the end of the problems each person may have a better idea of how his or her mind behaves.

Solution to the Second Two-Bottle Problem

Had the problem been presented on its own without the preceding problems, solution might have been quite difficult. Coming as it does immediately after the first two-bottle problem, solution should be easy.

The arrangement of the knives is shown on page 51. It is remarkable that three knives should be enough when at least two of them must be used to attain the required length.

The structure is far more stable than the four-knife bridge in the last problem. The position for placing the glass is shown by the coloured dotted outline in the figure, as it might not otherwise be obvious. The weight of the glass actually rests on the unsupported knife. This means that there can be no doubt about the weight of the knife being sufficient to balance the glass of water.

The angular nature of the bridge makes it easier to balance the structure than in the last problem, even if the knives do not have flat-sided handles.

The problem can be solved by applying to the three-bottle problem exactly the same procedure that was applied to the four-bottle problem in order to make the four-knife bridge. The clue might be the number of knives, even if the asymmetry of the three-bottle problem does not suggest that part of it can be regarded as a bridge (whereas a bridge might have been discerned between the diagonally opposite bottles in the four-bottle situation).

If the upward support of any knife in the three-bottle problem is converted into a downward force by swinging the knife completely around, then the problem is solved as shown. To apply to one of the knives in the three-bottle problem exactly the same process applied to two of the knives in the four-bottle problem is surely not a great leap in thinking.

The bridge does not run in a straight line between its supports, and this unusual angular form may have deterred some who considered what would happen if one of the supports in the three-bottle problem were removed. It is only when the altered position of the third knife is considered and the possibility of balancing the glass of water on this becomes apparent that the solution can proceed.

In this case the direct application of a specific procedure that had been successful in solving another problem would have solved this one very rapidly. The application of the general principle of substituting a weight for a support might also have been effective, but the process would not have been so straightforward.

Several different experiences have contributed to solving the problem in the way described. The derivation of the solution to the first two-bottle problem from that of the four-bottle problem had to be applied to the solution of the three-bottle problem. In effect the solutions of all three preceding problems contributed to this solution.

It may be argued that the solution to the problem would have been less trouble if derived from first principles rather than from experience. Some people may indeed have solved it this way. The ultimate simplicity of the solution, however, does not mean that it would have been easy to discover without the benefit of experience.

The problem might have been phrased: If two knives are used to span a gap between two bottles just over a knife's length apart, how can a third knife be used to fasten the other two into a structure strong enough to support a full glass of water? Stated in this way the problem would have been very difficult, even though the actual solution is simple.

The solution of this problem could give rise to the following comments:
1. The interaction of several separate experiences may be required for the solution of one problem.
2. A specific procedure used in solving another problem may be directly applied without using general principles.

3. An attempt to solve a problem should not be abandoned too early because it seems inappropriate, but the attempt should be seen as a whole.
4. The way a problem is presented may make a great difference to the ease with which it is solved.

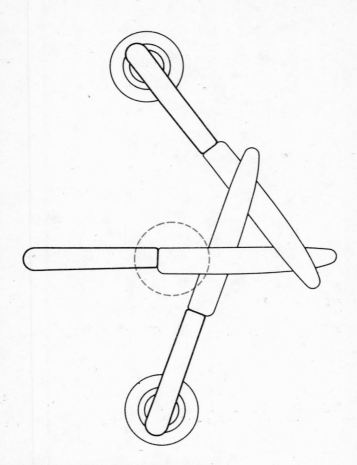

Solution to the Second Two-Bottle Problem

PROBLEM 5

Construct a stable platform on top of a single bottle using all
four knives. No part of any knife may touch the ground.
Place a full glass of water on the platform. The platform must,
however, be stable before the addition of the glass.

In the course of trying to solve the problems some people may try several different arrangements of the knives, whereas others may try only a few. This depends on the imagination of the problem-solver or on the method chosen. To try out different ideas one after the other and still have more to try out may eventually lead to a solution. On the other hand, an abundance of ideas may confuse the development of a logical approach.

The difference between someone who seems to have masses of ideas to try out and someone who does not seem to have any may not lie in their imaginations. A person who logically criticizes his ideas at an early stage may find that very few of them get through to a trying-out stage. This may seem an economy in time and effort, yet a cursory logical examination may easily reject an effective idea. Moreover, new ideas often arise from the failure of other ideas. A certain arrangement of the knives may not work, but a modification of this may lead on to quite a different arrangement, one that may never have been reached if the original idea had been logically rejected as it deserved to be. Experimentation with unsuccessful ideas is as much a source of experience as the demonstration of the final solution.

An increasing familiarity with the materials of a problem, in this case the knives, can best be acquired by handling them. There must, however, be a point at which trial-and-error becomes uneconomical and direct logical methods take over. This point is determined by the cost, in time, in energy, and in everything else of each trial. In these knife problems, this point may be reached quite late, but in other problems it may come very early, especially if any trial is expensive.

The alternative to trying out ideas is to examine carefully past experience to see whether it contains anything which might be regarded as resembling a trial of the new idea. Even so, this may be misleading, and if the resemblance is imperfect a good idea may be lost.

It is the function of logic to derive from the environment rules for the environment. With such rules it should be possible to predict entirely within the mind whether a new idea will work. The worth of such rules depends both on the logical ability of the mind and the extent of its experience. Both the ability and experience of others can be borrowed from the medium of education. The application of the rules and their relevance remain a personal matter.

If there is a logical direction in which to proceed and the economics of trial-and-error are unfavourable, it would seem wise to proceed logically until logic proves ineffective. Where originality rather than competence is required the other method is preferable.

In working through these problems, the tendency of the mind to adopt the logical method, trial-and-error, or the chance method may become apparent. The ease with which a switch can be made from one method to the other can also be examined.

Solution to the One-Bottle Problem

There may be several other solutions to this problem in addition to the one shown on page 59. This gives an aerial view, the dotted grey circle indicating the rim of the bottle on which the entire structure is balanced. The structure is stable and easily supports a full glass of water at its centre.

This particular solution is shown because it follows directly from experience gained in previous problems. In both versions of the two-bottle problem the solution depended on the realization that a support could be replaced by the downward force of a knife handle. This involved changing the position of one or two knives. The same principle can be applied to the whole structure involved in the solution to the four-bottle problem. In this problem there was a structure supported by four bottles and bearing a weight at its centre. If the structure is inverted, the weight at the centre becomes the single supporting bottle, and the weight of the knives themselves replaces the four supporting bottles.

In the previous problem a specific procedure which had proved useful proves so again. In contrast, the solution to this problem requires the changing of the specific procedure back into more general terms.

The same solution could have been derived directly from the
four-bottle problem even if there had been no experience of
either two-bottle problem. This could have been done by anyone
who could see the four-bottle structure not in terms of the
weight of a glass of water and the support of four bottles, but
simply as two sets of forces one acting at the centre of the
structure and others acting in the opposite direction at each
corner.

This is another instance of the immense value of the ability to get
beyond the obvious appearances of things and look at them in
different ways.

Many people may have solved the problem as a fresh one without
calling on any direct experience gained from the previous
problems except perhaps a certain dexterity with the knives.
Such an approach may have been just as effective in terms of
finding a solution, but the ability to profit from experience has
not been shown.

It may be argued that, if the four-bottle problem had not
previously been regarded as a matter of forces acting in opposite
directions, at the time it was experienced, it was unlikely to be
so regarded in retrospect. To interpret a solution in terms of
past experience is not the same as arriving at that solution
through past experience.

This is true and emphasizes the usefulness of appreciating as fully as possible the significance of the experience at the time and not just its immediate usefulness.

It is always possible to search through relevant experience and seek to establish some connexion with the problem of the moment.

Even if the connexion between the solution to the four-bottle problem and the solution to the one-bottle problem can only be made by hindsight, it is still worth making, for it emphasizes a general principle that becomes part of experience and that may be useful later.

Comments on this section could include the following:
1. If looked at in the right way, experience continues to yield far more information than is at first apparent.
2. The usefulness of specific principles may sometimes obscure the general principles that can be derived from them.
3. It is more useful to appreciate the full significance of experiences as they are acquired than to try to explore them in retrospect.
4. Dealing with an experience can itself provide a further experience.

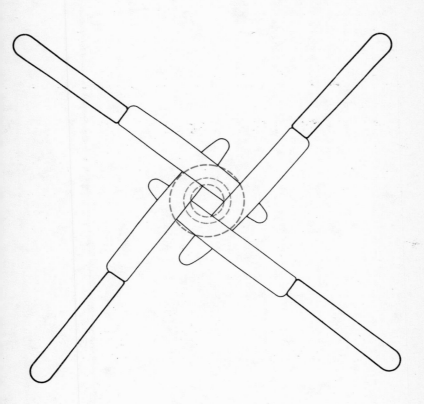

Solution to the One-Bottle Problem

This course has been offered as an opportunity to think and to become conscious of the thinking process. As the course proceeded, increasing practice should have made this awareness more informative.

The series of five problems was intended to be simple in solution and yet to demand a certain skill in thinking. The solutions did not depend on special knowledge and were easy to understand once they had been demonstrated.

Each problem considered separately might have been quite difficult. As a series, the experience derived from the previous problems could have made the later solutions simple, if maximum use was being made of the experience. In this way, it was hoped to exercise not only the faculty of problem-solving, but also that of handling experience, since the latter is so important a part of thinking.

Throughout, comments have been set down as no more than suggestions offered to stimulate personal observations of a similar sort. Doing something is much better than merely listening, since opinions can be formed on a personal experience basis.

THE SECOND 5-DAY COURSE IN THINKING

The Blocks: Sequential Thinking

Were it not too much bother you might deem it wise to do some physical exercise every day. With rather less bother you are offered an opportunity to amuse yourself with the mental exercise provided by the second five-day course in thinking.

As in the first course, the problems are in no sense a test. It matters little whether you solve them so long as you try them. Nor is there any hurry. You are probably capable of doing all the problems at one sitting. If you were to do this, a mild dose of self-satisfaction is all you would derive from the book. On the other hand, if you tackle the problems one a day as suggested, you will have time to mull over your own insights into the way you handled the problems and so gain more than self-satisfaction.

The comments offered are meant not to teach anything, but to suggest the sort of things you can so easily teach yourself simply by observing your mind in action. It is hoped that you may be amused by the course, for you will be taught nothing but the usefulness of teaching yourself. This method has the advantage of freeing you from the deficiencies of the teacher.

In some ways the problems used here are similar to those used in the first course; in other ways they are deliberately different.

As before, no experience at all is required, nor is any specialized knowledge an advantage. As before, each problem is complete in itself and at the same time is part of a series. A series provides an opportunity for handling experience, a very necessary part of thinking. The main difference from the bottle problems is the abundance of possible approaches. With the bottle problems you could do little until you hit on the right approach. With the block problems it is so easy to try a new approach that it is difficult to sit still and do nothing.

The first and second courses overlap to some extent. Since no deliberate effort is required, it is hoped that the gentle method of repetition will suffice to underline those few points that seem worth underlining and so commit them painlessly to your memory. The courses may also be used separately, and there is no need to dutifully plough through them one after the other.

Whereas the problems in the first course seemed to require a sudden 'insight' solution, the problems in the second course can be solved by a sequence of ideas or successive modifications of an idea – sequential thinking.

Equipment

All that is required are six block-shaped objects of equal size. Any of the following items could provide such blocks:
Books (of equal size and thickness; paperbacks would be best)
Cigarette packets

Matchboxes
Cereal boxes
Detergent boxes
The cereal boxes are ideal, especially if they are intact and unused. Sugar lumps are not recommended on account of their smallness and unevenness.

The Problems

Each problem requires that the six blocks be arranged in accordance with certain requirements. These requirements consist of the way in which the blocks touch one another. The rules governing the arrangements are as follows:

1. A block is said to touch another block when some flat surface or part of a flat surface of one block is in contact with a flat surface or part of a flat surface of the other block. Contact through an edge or corner does not count. In the diagram below the two blocks are not considered to be touching.

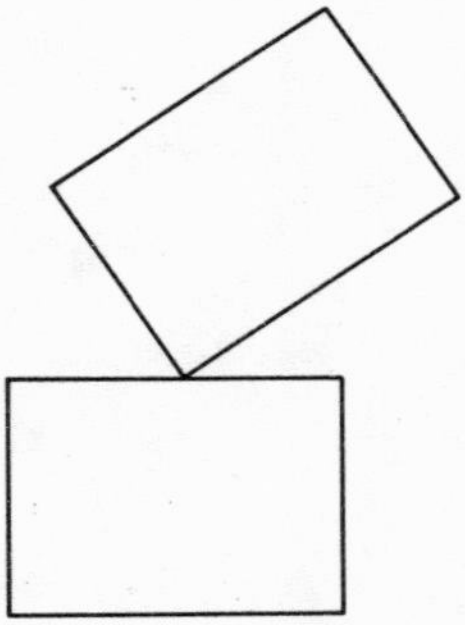

2. The arrangement must be self-supporting. That is to say, the arrangement of blocks must stand by itself and keep its shape. Any arrangement which requires the support of a hand or any other object does not qualify.

Since the reader is the only judge of the correctness of a solution (it is only possible to illustrate some of the solutions), it is necessary to examine very carefully any arrangement that is offered as a solution to the problem. It is all too easy to offer as correct a solution which is not. When I was trying out the problems on different people I was always being offered solutions that turned out to be wrong on close examination. In order to be sure that the solutions are absolutely correct it is suggested that *each block be taken in turn and its contacts counted*. This point does need emphasizing, for to accept an incorrect solution is the most serious of errors since it cannot be detected.

PROBLEM 1

Arrange the six blocks so that each touches two and only two other blocks.

The problem is not difficult, and there are several possible solutions. If one solution is found with ease, then the other solutions can be sought. There is an aesthetic satisfaction in finding the simplest possible solution, a beauty in economy of effort. Since many of the problems do have alternative solutions, you may choose to exercise your taste for beauty in addition to your desire for effectiveness.

Different people will use different approaches to the problem. All are satisfactory if they prove effective and provide a solution. The most important thing, however, is not the solution, but an awareness of how it is reached.

The solution may come about so suddenly that you may not be aware of how it was reached. You can, nevertheless, be aware of the setting in which the solution came about.

Some people may sit and stare at the blocks for a few moments and then reach out and arrange them in the correct pattern. The logical road to the solution may be so obvious that there is little hesitation. Other people may prefer to play with the blocks until a correct solution turns up. This chance method can be very effective. The correct solution itself may turn up or else an arrangement so nearly correct that all that is required is a slight modification. This method seems effortless. As long as the blocks are moved around into new patterns there is a chance of something happening. To keep playing around and generating new patterns is easy with the blocks, but with many other problems it can be difficult.

The second part of the chance method is careful examination of what turns up. Each new arrangement, since it comes about by chance, must be carefully assessed to see whether it is a solution or close to a solution. The rapidity and accuracy with which this examination can be carried out may make all the difference between the success and failure of the chance method. Too slow or too careless an assessment would make the method very inefficient. I have often seen people produce a correct solution by chance and then reject it through faulty examination.

You may feel insulted at the suggestion that a chance method should be used to solve a problem. It seems a poor substitute for logic and reason. Alternatively you may maintain that it is not really a chance method at all.

A true chance method might involve dropping the blocks out of the window in the hope that they might form a correct pattern on the ground outside. The chances of this happening would be small. So one imposes certain limits within which chance is to act. The first limit might be that the blocks are to be dropped within the room. The second limit might be that the blocks be dropped on the table. In spite of these two limits the chances of obtaining a correct solution in this manner are still tiny – all that has really been increased is the convenience of the procedure. The next limit imposed is that all the blocks should touch one another. This means that they must be moved around by hand instead of being dropped. It remains a chance process (there is no planned pattern), but the possibility of success is quite high. This possibility can be increased by putting further limits, but that could have dangerous consequences as will be seen later.

It may be that by this time you have become determined to use the superior logical method rather than a chance one. Indeed you may already have worked out at least one solution.

Solution to Problem 1

A solution to this problem is shown on page 75. This solution
or variations of it will be the one obtained by most people. It
is a solution that is easy to reach by purely logical means.

One approach is to consider a pattern in which each block has
two neighbours, one in front and one behind. The obvious
answer is a circle.

Another approach is to arrange the blocks in some simple
pattern and then try and modify this to give the solution. Such
a pattern could be a row of six blocks. In a row, each block
except the end ones has two neighbours, the end ones have
only one neighbour. The end blocks can be brought into
contact with each other by bending the row into a circle, and
then the problem is solved since all the blocks touch two and
only two others.

A much more unusual solution is shown on page 76. Anyone
who achieved this solution may congratulate himself on a
certain originality of mind. The peculiar feature about this
arrangement is that you would be very unlikely to reach it by
the chance method. As described earlier, one of the limits
imposed on the chance arrangements was that all the blocks

should be touching. This limit is necessary if there is to be any hope of success. In this solution the blocks are not all touching but are separated into two distinct groups. The danger of the chance method is that the path to a solution may lie outside the self-imposed limits, for these limits are no more than a guess in the direction of the solution.

There are a number of other possible solutions. For instance, the circle may be constructed in the vertical plane by building a 'doorway' out of the blocks. In essence such an arrangement is no different from the circle one shown in the first solution.

The obvious advantage of the circle solution over the other one is that the circle solution establishes a principle that can be used to arrange any number of blocks so that each touches two others. The two three-groups solution on the other hand is unique for six blocks. To have derived a general principle may have advantages in the future.

Comments on the first day might run as follows:
1. The chance method is a perfectly valid method of looking for a solution.
2. The chance method involves the generating of many possible approaches to the problem and the rapid assessment of each new approach.
3. To increase the likelihood of success, certain limits are imposed within which chance is to act.

4. The establishment of limits for the chance arrangements may shut out a worthwhile solution.
5. A logical approach may be reliable and effective, but may not lead to an original solution.
6. The discovery of a general principle that can be applied to future situations may have advantages over the use of a solution only suited to the current problem.

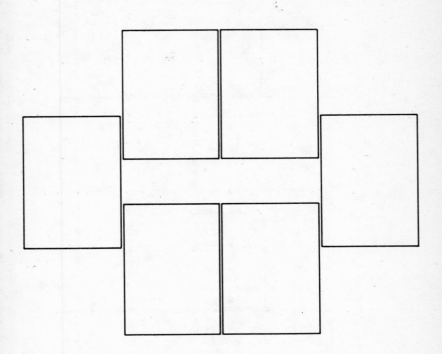

First Solution to Problem 1

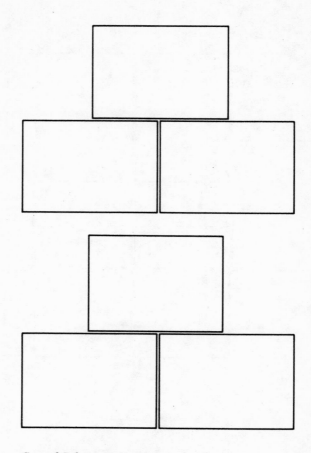

Second Solution to Problem 1

PROBLEM 2

Arrange the six blocks so that each touches three and only three others.

The useful difference between Problems 1 and 2 is that one comes after the other. The many uses of experience were outlined in the first five-day course, but there can be no harm in suggesting that you make your own additions to the list offered overleaf.

The first use of experience is to give confidence. Although unjustified (since the first problem was so easy), such confidence may very well make the other problems easier.

The second use of experience is as a museum for mistakes. This hardly applies in this instance, since none should have been made in tackling the first problem.

The third use of experience is as a source of principles. Such principles might only be general ways of handling a problem or they might be much more specific and include solutions to particular types of problem.

The fourth use of experience is to provide arrangements of blocks which can be modified into a solution for the current problem.

How much do you rely on experience? How much do you attempt to use it deliberately? These are probably matters of individual taste and temperament. In many ways experience exerts its effects even when deliberately ignored. Mistakes are not likely to be repeated even when no attempt is made to recall them. On the other hand, a search for a past arrangement to serve as a suitable starting point for solution of the present problem is deliberate.

The modifying method is part of most problem-solving attempts. You may use it from the outset or only after some other method has brought you near enough to the final solution for you to be able to concentrate on the remaining difference. The method is really no more than a focusing of attention on this difference followed by attempts to reduce it. When a suitable starting arrangement can be provided by experience, the modifying method can be used from the beginning.

You may wish to ignore the arrangements experienced in the first problem, or you may wish to use one of them as a convenient starting point. Either way, the choice will now be a deliberate, self-conscious one.

Solution to Problem 2

The solutions shown here may have been reached by pure logical effort, by the modifying method, or by chance. The description of the approach given here suggests a logical progression that is easy to outline after the problem has been solved, but not so easy to use for solving the problem.

The solution on page 83 might have been reached by the modifying method. In the circle arrangement (see page 75), two opposite blocks might have been removed from the long sides and the end block moved in to give an arrangement of four blocks each of which touches two others. In this way the problem is divided into two parts: first arrange four blocks so that each touches two others; second add the two other blocks so that each block touches three others.

The two additional blocks are placed across the opposite junctions of the four-block arrangement so that each block in this arrangement now touches three other blocks. The additional blocks are then brought into contact with one another, and thus each touches three other blocks and the problem is solved.

An alternative and more elegant solution which is also much easier arises out of the second solution to Problem 1. This solution (see page 76) consisted of two three-groups in which each block touches two others. If one such group is placed directly on top of the other, each block touches its two neighbours as before, but in addition touches another block either above or below itself (see page 84). The same solution could also have been achieved by pushing together three piles of two blocks. It is curious that the solution which had seemed less useful (since it provided no general principle) should turn out to be more useful. This could never have been predicted at the time. It does sometimes happen that a fortunate choice of solution provides quite undeserved benefits later.

A few people may have come up with the solution shown on page 85. This solution is interesting, for, as you may at once notice, it can be derived by either of the approaches mentioned above. Looked at in one way, the arrangement consists of two three-groups (this time in the vertical plane) pushed up against each other. On the other hand, you may prefer to look at it as an arrangement of four blocks each of which touches two others, since corner contacts do not count. This arrangement is then modified by the addition of two other blocks.

In place of these suggested solutions you may have come up with something quite different, something that is weird or more elegant.

Comments on the second day might include the following:
1. It may sometimes prove useful to divide a problem up and tackle one part after another.
2. It may be just as easy to start from scratch as to modify a previously used arrangement.
3. A fortunate choice of solution at one point may make things much easier later on.
4. Apparently different solutions may not really be different at all.
5. The same solution may be reached in two completely different ways.

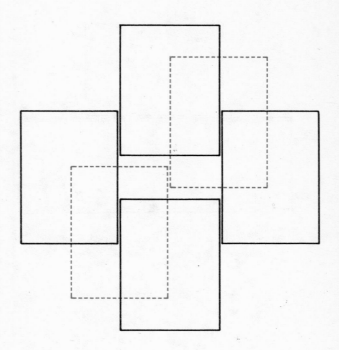

First Solution to Problem 2

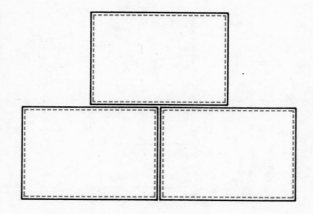

Second Solution to Problem 2

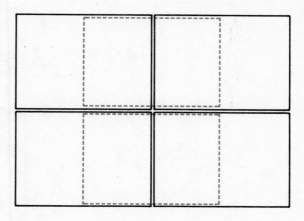

Third Solution to Problem 2

PROBLEM 3

Arrange the six blocks so that each touches four and only four others.

Why is it that problems take any time at all to solve? Why is it that you cannot stretch out your hand and arrange the blocks in the correct pattern without any hesitation – as some people may have done for Problem 1?

The block problems are exactly opposite to the bottle problems in one important respect: each type illustrates one aspect of why problems take some time to be solved.

With the bottle problems it was difficult to make any progress at all until the complete solution turned up almost in a flash of inspiration. It was a matter of waiting for the right idea, waiting for the right approach to the problem to crystallize. There were not many different approaches to be tried out.

With the block problems it is different. It is extremely easy to try new ideas with the blocks since it is only a matter of moving the blocks around. There is no question of waiting for ideas. On the contrary, the difficulty with the block problems is that it is too easy to get started. As a result wrong directions are easily taken. Having taken a wrong direction, you move away from the solution instead of towards it. If the initial choice of arrangement is wrong, the problem may become harder to solve. With the block problems you are embarrassed by the abundance of possible approaches. How can you be certain of making the right start?

At the outset every approach seems right. Although all the steps may not be clear there is always a feeling of anticipation, anticipation that this must be the path to the solution. Should the path peter out or progress become blocked, there follows a brief period of desolation until a new approach suggests itself. Enthusiasm returns, for surely the new approach must be the right one. And so it is for each new approach.

At some stage in the solution of these problems you will find that all your efforts to solve the problems with the blocks lying flat on the table seem to come to nought. Suddenly you will have the brilliant new idea that the blocks must be stood on end. The newness of this idea seems the key to the problem. There is no good reason to suppose that the blocks on end are better, and yet the very newness of the approach suffices to make success seem certain. Many people also feel that somehow the problems cannot be solved in an obvious way (otherwise they would not be set), and hence the idea of putting the blocks on end has a certain value simply because it is not obvious.

I once watched someone solve the entire series of problems using the blocks on end. There was absolutely no advantage to be gained by doing it in this manner. All it meant was that he was using blocks of a different shape (higher and much narrower). With such blocks it was possible to do everything that could be done with the flat blocks, but it was much more difficult. This performance provided a good example of the dangers of the barely adequate approach. An approach that does give a solution, albeit with much difficulty, may go on being used. Unless you are exceptional you would not like to abandon a proved approach in order to look for a better one. Thus early success may be an eventual disadvantage.

It is hoped that this discussion on the use of the blocks on end will not deter you from using the blocks in this way should there seem to be any advantage in so doing. Despite the above comments, newness of an approach is always sufficient justification for trying it.

Solution to Problem 3

The solution shown on page 93 is an obvious descendant of a solution to the previous problem (see page 84) and that solution was in turn descended from a previous solution. All three solutions are based on the use of the fundamental three-group. This is a basic approach to the problem, and you may or may not choose to call it a general principle.

It is possible to derive this solution from the second solution to Problem 2 in a purely logical manner. You may actually have done so, or you may now find it flattering to assume that you had really proceeded in this manner.

In the former each block touched its two neighbours in the three-group and also another block (above or below). In order to satisfy the requirements of Problem 3, all that needs to be done is to get each block to touch two others above or below itself. This is what has been achieved in this solution to Problem 3.

For my own part I derived the solution to Problem 3 from the second solution to Problem 2 in a much less logical but probably more honest manner. In order to solve Problem 3, I deliberately chose the former arrangement and then just looked at it for a while. Then I thought it would be interesting

to see what would happen if I reversed the top three-group.
This was purely in the spirit of playing around, of trying
something new for its own sake. Once the top group was turned
around and shifted slightly so that it would balance, the
problem turned out to be solved. This was a chance-and-play
modification of a previous solution and not a logical approach.
Those who preferred to avoid the three-group approach may
have arrived at the solution shown on page 94. At once it will
be noticed that the two side blocks are indeed standing on end.
There are many ways this particular solution could have been
reached, and the one suggested below may or may not have
been used.

One way of arranging one block to touch four others is to
arrange the four in a tight group as shown on page 85, and
then sit the block on top of the group covering the junction.
In such an arrangement the top block touches four others and
the rest touch three others. Five blocks are used. The obvious
next step (it may not be so obvious except in hindsight) is to
put the sixth block *underneath* the junction, and thus it
touches four others and the rest now touch $3+1=4$.
Unfortunately this structure is difficult to balance, and one of
the rules is that the solution arrangements be self-supporting.
To achieve this the whole thing is turned on its side or rather
reconstructed in the vertical plane. If the arrangement on
page 94 is looked at from the side, it can be seen that the side
blocks 'cap' an arrangement of four other blocks, one cap on
each side.

Comments on the third day:

1. A problem may be difficult to solve because of a lack of ideas or because of an abundance of ideas. Choice of the wrong direction can lead away from the solution.
2. The newness of an approach is sufficient justification for trying it.
3. Attempts should be made to exchange a barely adequate approach for a better one.
4. A general type of approach that has been successful in previous problems is always worth trying again.
5. Modification of a previous solution by chance-and-play methods may be just as effective as logical modification (the let's-see-what-happens-if policy).
6. An attempt to solve a problem part by part may be effective.

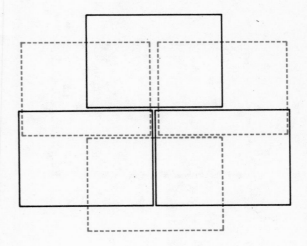

First Solution to Problem 3

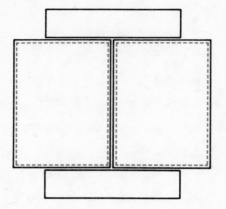

Second Solution to Problem 3

PROBLEM 4

Arrange the six blocks so that each touches five others.

This problem is not easy. If you solve it with ease, you may congratulate yourself on the brilliance of your thinking. If you have difficulty in solving it, you may console yourself with the thought that almost everyone else will have just as much difficulty.

In solving the problem you may choose to use a logical or a chance method. You may choose to modify a previous solution or start from the beginning. It is important either to choose an approach deliberately or else to be aware of the approach into which you drift.

Although the chance method may be the more effortless, it may also be tedious in that you have to examine each arrangement. One way of assessing the validity of an arrangement is to carefully count the contacts of each block, one after another. Such an assessment is absolutely *essential* before any arrangement is offered as a solution. It may, however, speed things up considerably to have some simpler preliminary test. This simple test could be used on the

arrangements generated by chance and the fuller test used only
if the arrangement passes the simpler screening test. The
screening test could take the form of a single condition that has
to be fulfilled or a single condition that has to be avoided. If
you intend to use the chance method, you could design such
a test for yourself. It is worth the effort, for the use of such a
test can speed up random thinking very much; in a situation
where ideas come freely it is their assessment that takes time.

Although you may be reluctant to use the chance method, it
is worth remembering that this method has one particular
advantage over the logical one: much of the difficulty in
solving these block problems arises from starting out in the
wrong direction, and the chance method is the method of no
direction. By definition any move in it is independent of the
previous moves (in contrast to the logical method).
Nevertheless you will persist in thinking that the chance
method is inferior and the resort of those whose logic is
inadequate to handle the problem.

Logic may not be the best way to handle a problem for quite
another reason. Sometimes a point is reached in problem-
solving when a completely new idea is required. No amount of
effort along the old lines will suffice to solve the problem.
Since the idea is completely new, it cannot be derived from
what has been done before. Logic can no more provide such
an idea than you can raise yourself by tugging on your
bootlaces. It is only fair to add, however, that what may seem

a completely new idea to one person may be derived logically
by someone else who is looking at the problem in a different
way.

Solution to Problem 4

Before proceeding to the solution, let us examine a very rapid screening test that could have been applied to all tentative arrangements. Since there are six blocks and each must touch five others, the requirement is simply that each block must touch *all* the others. Thus any arrangement in which any two blocks are separated *must* be wrong. This is a very quick test to apply and very much less bother than counting the contacts of each block.

The two approaches described below are more or less logical
in nature. This is not to suggest that the chance method is
ineffective, but that there is nothing to describe about it. To
some extent even the logical method is trial-and-error at some
stage.

In problem-solving the usual tendency is to try to alter the
starting situation until it becomes the desired end situation –
the solution. It is often helpful to reverse the end situation
towards the starting situation.

If one block is set aside, the problem is to arrange the
remaining five blocks so that each touches all the others. This
is the first part of the problem. The second is to add the sixth
block so that it touches all the blocks in the five-block
arrangement. Thus it touches five blocks, and all the others
will touch $4+1=5$. To solve this altered problem the basic
three-group is used as a start. One block is laid across the
junction to give a four-block arrangement in which each block
touches three others. The fifth block is now added to touch all
the others. This cannot in fact be done without a new idea.

The new idea is to use the blocks diagonally. Previously all the
arrangements have used the natural and symmetrical way of
arranging blocks, that is, with all the edges parallel or at right
angles and each block set squarely with respect to the others.
Usually the diagonal idea arises through playing around with
the blocks on top of the three-group as you try to get each to

touch all three below. You may prefer to pretend to have reached it by more logical means.

Once the five-group has been arranged (see page 102), the solution is reached by adding the sixth block to make a three-group with the blocks on top and then moving this group around until each top block touches all the bottom ones. In fact, all that is necessary is to slide the two blocks towards the top of the page and then add the sixth block.

A completely different approach would be to consider that in one plane the greatest number of blocks that can meet at one junction (so that each touches all the others) is three. This gives the already familiar three-group. If one three-group is laid on top of another three-group (as in solutions to Problems 2 and 3), the procedure is to arrange the junctions of the groups in the appropriate manner. The attention has been shifted from the blocks themselves to their junctions (T-shaped junctions). This shift of attention can often be the clue to solving a problem. The blocks themselves need no longer be used since they are now more of a hindrance than a help. One T junction is drawn on a piece of paper and then a second T junction is drawn over it so that the lines of the top T cut those of the bottom T at four points. This means that each block in the top group lies across two junctions of the bottom group and hence three blocks. Such an arrangement is shown on page 103.

The final solution to Problem 4 is shown on page 104.

*The
Fourth
Day*

Comments on the fourth day might include:

1. A quick screening test for the usefulness of any new approach can speed up problem-solving considerably, especially when the chance method is being used.
2. Sometimes a completely new idea may be required before the problem can be solved.
3. A new idea cannot be logically derived from the old idea, but must come from outside or by chance.
4. In solving a problem, it often makes things easier to change the end situation backward towards the starting one as well as changing the starting one towards the end one.
5. Even though a logical method is used, there may still be times when the next step is achieved by playing with the materials.
6. A shift of attention from one aspect of the situation to another may lead to a solution.
7. Pencil-and-paper planning may still be useful, even if the problem is capable of being tackled directly.

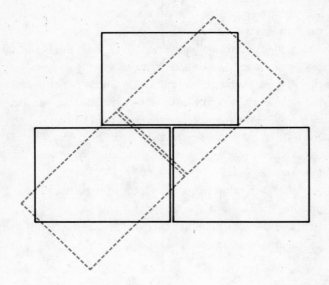

The Five-Group

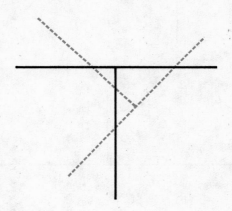

The T Junction

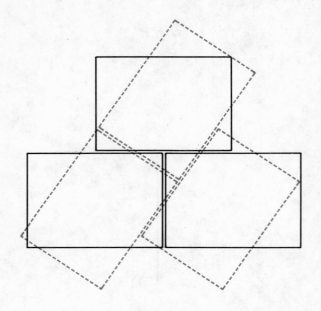

Solution to Problem 4

PROBLEM 5

Arrange the six blocks in the following fashion:
one block must touch only one other
one block must touch only two others
one block must touch only three others
one block must touch only four others
one block must touch only five others

This problem seems much more complicated than the previous
problems. In actual fact, there are fewer conditions to be
fulfilled than with the other problems, since the relationships of
only five blocks are defined, whereas in the previous problems
conditions were laid down for all six blocks. The major change
is that the requirements for each block are different instead of
being all the same. Whether this makes the problem easier or
more difficult is a matter for you to decide or, rather, find out.

At first sight the problem seems suited to a stage-by-stage
approach. The staging method is nothing more than a name
for the way most people usually tackle a problem. The
requirements of the problem are satisfied one after another,
and, when the last one has been ticked off the list, the problem
has been solved. Whenever there are many requirements or the
problem seems complicated this often does seem the best

approach. You may, however, prefer to tackle such problems as a whole, directing your attention not to breaking them down into parts, but to simplifying them while keeping them intact.

The drawback of the staging method is that some problems cannot be tackled piece by piece. When all the parts of the solution are interrelated, it is not possible to build up the solution bit by bit. The bottle problems are of this nature.

Another disadvantage of the staging method is that the order in which the stages are tackled may be crucial. If they are tackled in the wrong order, solution may prove difficult or even impossible. Nor is the correct order for the stages necessarily the most obvious one.

Instead of the staging method, you may prefer to try the simplifying method. This may mean looking at the problem in different ways until it becomes less complicated.

Problem 5 appears unrelated to the previous problems. Apart from a general facility in handling the blocks, experience may provide no help.

Solution to Problem 5

If you used the staging method, your steps may have gone
something as follows:

first requirement:	one block to touch only one other
first stage:	put down one block and then another one to touch it
second requirement:	one block to touch only two others
second stage:	there are two blocks on the table so put down a further block to touch both of them

Unfortunately, in satisfying the second requirement the first
requirement has been undone. This is the sort of confusion
that can arise. You yourself may have avoided this simple
mistake and may have proceeded to solve the problem by
careful selection of the order of the stages, but this confusion
does arise quite often when the staging method is used.

A different way to use the staging method is to ignore the six
blocks and start with just three. The problem is now to arrange
these three blocks so that the contacts are 1 and 2. The
answer is obviously a simple row of three blocks where the
middle block touches 2 and the end block touches 1. The next

stage is to add a fourth block so that the list of contacts becomes 1, 2, and 3. This can be done very simply as shown on page 111. The next stage is to add a fifth block so that the contacts come to be 1, 2, 3 and 4. Again this is very simple and can be done as shown on page 112. The final stage is to add the sixth block so that the contacts come to be 1, 2, 3, 4 and 5. This final stage is as straightforward as the previous stages and gives the solution to Problem 5 as shown on page 113. Approached in this methodical way the problem seems extremely easy.

Instead of using this staging method you may have preferred to try and modify a previous solution. One interesting way of doing this would be to take the solution to Problem 4 (see page 104) and try to modify it by subtraction. Since in this arrangement all blocks touch five others, the idea is to diminish the contacts progressively until they become 1, 2, 3, 4 and 5. As a start, one block would be taken off the top layer and placed against a block in the lower layer. This lower block would still touch five others, but the rest would now only touch four. Then a second block would be taken off the top and placed so that the block touching five others would continue to do so and another block would continue to touch four others. The remaining block touches three others. The blocks that have been moved touch one and two, and so the problem is solved. The final arrangement is shown on page 114. In this figure the block remaining on top has been realigned to cover the junction squarely. Thus, by moving only two blocks the

solution to Problem 4 has been changed into a solution for
Problem 5.

There are very many other ways of solving this particular
problem. It is interesting to follow the evolution of your own
particular solution and to wonder whether the approaches
suggested here would have occurred to you and, if not, why not.
You may possibly have found an approach that is better than
those suggested here, but that is unlikely in this instance.

For those who pay heed to the comments, the list for the final
day might be as follows:

1. Complicated problems can sometimes be solved piece by
   piece. Each requirement is satisfied in turn, until the complete
   solution is achieved. This could be called the 'staging
   method'.
2. Where the solution consists of interrelated parts the problem
   cannot be solved by the staging method.
3. In the staging method the sequence of the stages may be
   crucial. Use of an incorrect sequence can lead to confusion.
   The correct sequence may not be the obvious one.
4. An attempt may be made to look at a complicated problem
   from many different points of view in the hope that it may
   be resolved into a simpler problem.
5. The solution to a complicated problem may be progressively
   built up from the solution to a much simpler problem.

6. Even though the new problem seems quite unrelated to previous ones, it may be worth trying to modify a previous solution.
7. Modification by subtraction consists in taking the solution to a more difficult problem and then simplifying it.

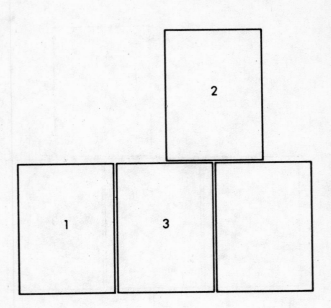

Contacts 1, 2, and 3

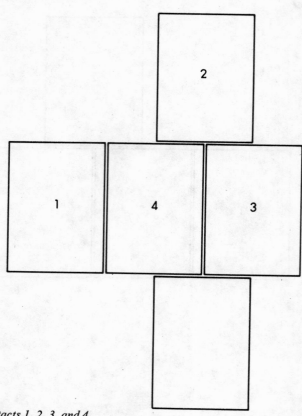

Contacts 1, 2, 3, and 4

*The
Fifth
Day*

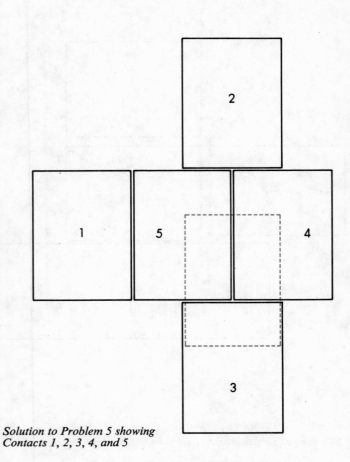

*Solution to Problem 5 showing
Contacts 1, 2, 3, 4, and 5*

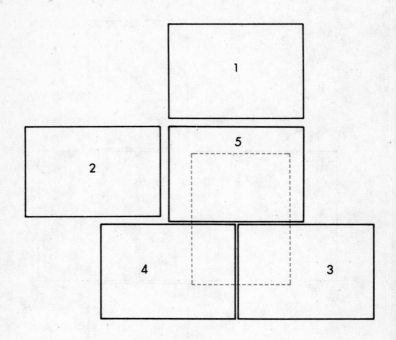

Solution to Problem 5 as derived from Solution to Problem 4

In tackling and solving the problems you may have come to the conclusion that thinking is a rather messy business. You may have used approaches as neatly logical as those suggested in the text, or you may suspect that such approaches were really developed after the problem had already been solved. If your particular approach was messy but nevertheless effective, you may have obtained a more honest insight into the way you think than if you were to dress up your achievement in a respectable logical garb.

Logic is swift and immensely effective (except in the field of new ideas). Unfortunately the logical method is not the way problems are usually tackled. Practical thinking is far removed from the nice purity of academic reasoning. There is a huge admixture of experience, whim, belief, chance, and play. It is interesting that for some problems it is necessary to programme electronic computers in this only partially logical mode of behaviour.

Since this messy business of thinking seems to be a skill rather than a mathematical ability, it ought to be possible to improve it by exercises and self-observation as in these courses.

THE THIRD 5-DAY COURSE
IN THINKING

The L Game: Strategic Thinking

There was not quite so much fun to be had with the block problems as with the bottle problems. This third course has to do with a game that may seem too simple to be possible. With the previous types of problem any effective solution was acceptable. It is true that you were exhorted to find not any old solution but the neatest and most elegant one, but that was only a matter of exhortation and no one pays too much attention to that.

The third course is concerned with the sort of problem for which you can very easily find a solution, but are required to find the best possible solution. This type of problem occurs quite often in competitive situations. The new L game provides a convenient basis for the course. As before, no previous experience or special knowledge is required (nor is it possible in this case).

Unlike the previous fixed problems, game situations are always changing and it is more a matter of developing guiding principles than of solving each problem situation. This could be called strategic thinking.

The L Game

This game was designed by the author because he enjoys
playing games and yet hates to concentrate on a large number
of pieces. The intention was to produce the simplest possible
game that could still be played with a high degree of skill. An
attempt was made to fulfil the following conditions:

1. A minimum number of playing pieces, preferably one each.
2. The smallest possible board.
3. A game with very few rules, one that would be very simple
   to learn and to play.
4. A game that could be played with a high degree of skill.
5. A game that would not be determinate. A determinate game,
   such as nim or noughts and crosses, is one in which the
   starting player could always win if he knew the strategy. An
   indeterminate game is one which two perfect players would
   play forever.

The L game was the result. Each player has only one L piece.
The board is four squares by four squares. The game is easier to
learn and to play than noughts and crosses and yet can be played
with a high degree of skill. Against opponents who knew the
game, I myself have played for over an hour. Skill is required
because there are so many possible moves. There are over
18,000 positions for the pieces on the small board and at any
one moment there may be as many as 195 different moves of
which only one is successful.

Rules of the L Game

PIECES

Each player has an L-shaped piece, which covers four squares. In addition there are two small square neutral pieces which do not belong to the players but can be moved by either of them. Each neutral piece covers only one square.

STARTING POSITIONS

The diagram on the next page shows the disposition of the pieces on the board at the start of the game.

MOVES

Each player in turn must move his L piece to a new position. The piece may be picked up, turned around, turned right over, etc., and then placed back on the board in any new position whatsoever. A position is deemed to be new even if only one of the squares covered by the piece has been changed. The piece may be placed anywhere on the board so long as it covers an exact arrangement of squares and does not overlap another piece.

After the L piece has been moved, a player may – if he so wishes – move *either* neutral piece to any unoccupied square on the board.

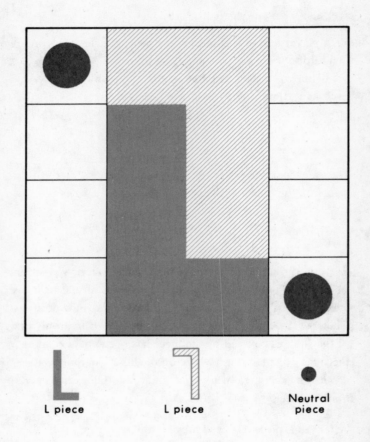

L piece   L piece   Neutral
                                  piece

The L Game – Starting Position

WINNING THE GAME

The object of the game is to force the opponent into a position from which he cannot move. The game is won when the opponent cannot change the position of his L piece. (The L piece must always be moved before a neutral piece is touched.)

The Problems

In this five-day course the L game is pictured in a simple form with grey circles representing the neutral pieces and the L pieces reduced in size to reveal the squares on which they lie. In all the problems the diagonally striped piece is assumed to belong to you, the reader, and the solid piece to me, the book.

The problems are simple enough and are intended to arouse the sort of considerations that might be employed while playing the game against an actual opponent.

PROBLEM 1

Below is shown the positions of the pieces at some stage in a
game. You have a choice of the three moves shown in pictures
A, *B*, *C*. The problem is to choose the best move.

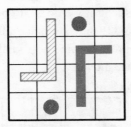

Game Setting

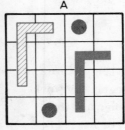
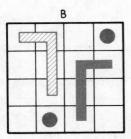
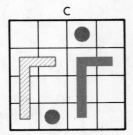

Choice of Moves

You are unlikely to feel that this is a difficult problem. But you may very well have a sense of awkwardness as you start to solve it. The situation is new, and there are no familiar criteria by which you could judge what action to take. Any move seems as easy as any other, and yet you sense, correctly, that some of the moves may be fatal.

The way the problem is presented simplifies the situation considerably, for you are restricted to a choice of only three moves. You only have to judge between these three possibilities. How much more difficult it would be if your choice were unlimited. You would then have to find all the possible moves and assess each. Below is a game position in which you have a choice of 195 possible moves.

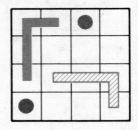

But even assessing three moves is awkward when you are so completely unfamiliar with the game. Presumably you would proceed by carrying out each move in your mind and then seeing what would happen. At first there will be a certain clumsiness in handling the pieces mentally, but your difficulties are more serious than this. By seeing what would happen if you were to make a certain move is meant seeing what the opponent would do, what counter move he would make. In this type of competitive situation you have to assume that the opponent is a perfect player and will make the best possible move. But how can you guess his moves when you cannot properly handle your own? This, then, is the major limitation in assessing your best move: not being able to predict the opponent's counter moves.

Realizing the above difficulty, you may decide to choose any move and then see what happens. In actual game-playing you might well use such a random policy deliberately in order to acquire familiarity with the game in general and certain moves in particular. Being on the wrong end of a winning move can be very instructive.

Solution to Problem 1

The counter move to each of the three possible moves is shown below. It may be seen that *C* was the best move. The other moves would have led to immediate defeat, as you will find if you try to move your L piece to a new position.

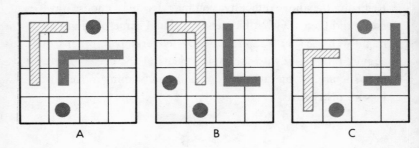

A   B   C

Counter Moves

Instant defeat may suggest that the game is very easy to win. In fact it is not. This sort of situation only arises when an experienced player is playing against a beginner. With two experienced players each player can assess his moves much better through being able to forecast his opponent's reaction. Neither player would choose a move that would lead to defeat – provided he had any choice and had not been trapped. When

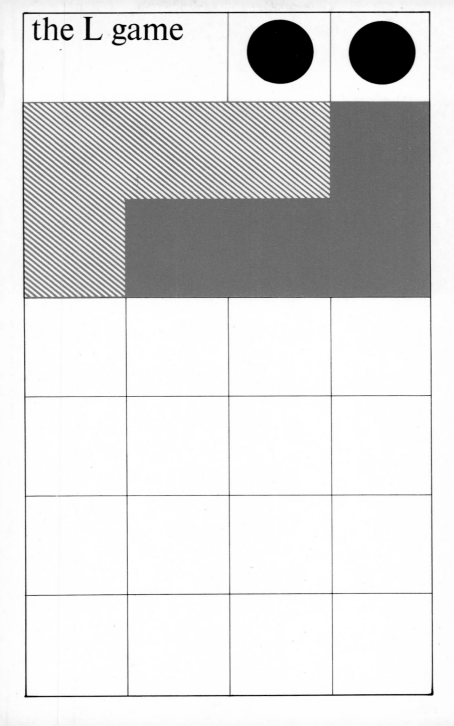

the L game

**The L game. Published in conjunction with
The Five-Day Course in Thinking by Edward de Bono
Penguin Books**

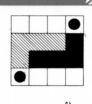

How to play the L game

Pieces

The board is made up of 16 squares. Each player (only 2 can play) has an L piece which he must move when it is his turn.

Object

The object of the game is to manoeuvre the other player into a position on the board where he cannot move his L piece.

Starting Position

Proceeding from the starting position, the first player
(and each player on each move thereafter) must move the L first.
When moving, a player may slide, turn or pick up and flip the L
into any open position other than the one it occupied prior to the
move. When the L has been moved, a player may move either one
(but only one) of the neutral square pieces to any open square
on the board. It is not required that the neutral piece
be moved, this is up to the player!
A player wins the game when his opponent cannot move his L piece.

two beginners are playing, the actual choice of moves is less
expert, but then so is the response to such a choice. One
beginner may make a mistake, but the other beginner may not
realize it is a mistake and may not know how to take advantage
of it to win the game.

Comments on the first day might include the following; you
may wish to add others of your own:
1. The value of a move is assessed by making it mentally and
   studying the consequences.
2. The consequences of a move depend on the opponent's
   ability. If the player's own ability is limited he cannot project
   any better skill on to the opponent, so the imagined
   consequences of a move may be very different from the real
   consequences.
3. To assess a move correctly it is necessary to suppose a
   perfect ability on the part of the opponent even if it does not
   exist.
4. Even though the opponent may have an almost perfect
   playing ability he may be prevented from using it by
   psychological manoeuvres.

PROBLEM 2

The disposition of the pieces at a given stage in a game is shown below. List all the possible moves open to you, and classify them under the following headings:

fatal: positions which would allow the opponent to win on the next move

weak: positions which, though not fatal, can lead to a fatal position; such positions put the player on the defensive

neutral: positions which do not offer any advantage to either player

strong: positions which are either outright winning positions or which force the opponent into an obvious weak position

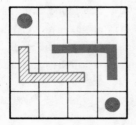

There are two extreme types of competitive situation. Most actual situations fall somewhere between these two extremes. The first type of situation is one where the possible moves are few and all of them are well known to each player. Success depends on anticipating the opponent's choice of move and misleading him about your own. The battle is essentially a psychological one.

In the second type of situation there is no need for psychology. This type of situation is very complex, and there are a great number of possible moves. Success depends on understanding the situation better than your opponent and so choosing the better moves. You may assume that the opponent will always make the best possible moves. How far short he falls of that ideal will be the measure of your success. Psychological methods need only be used when both players know all the possible moves so well that the situation has really reverted to the first type.

The L game falls into the second category. The number of possible moves is very large. A player who knows the moves thoroughly and can always see the implications of any move will do better than an opponent who cannot.

Solution to Problem 2

The total number of possible moves open to you in the game
setting shown on page 131 is 65.

These 65 possible moves may be classified as follows:
fatal :   22
weak: 17
neutral :   26
strong: 0

You may well have given up half-way through this problem,
finding it too difficult or too tedious. The way to do it would
be to find all the possible positions for your L piece first. For
each of these positions there are 13 possible positions for the
neutral pieces: no change in position plus 6 changes of
position for each of the pieces.

If you did work your way through the problem, it is likely that
your evaluation of the moves does not agree with that given
above. Without excluding the possibility that your evaluation
is a better one, it is reasonable to suggest that a more
experienced player may see counter moves which have escaped
your attention. Such counter moves would determine the
worth of any particular move.

Whether you finished the problem or not you will have been impressed by the difficulty and tediousness of this task. You would hardly be inclined to use such a procedure every time it was your turn to make a move.

The above method is the perfect way to play the L game or any game of this type. It is also perfectly impossible. To evaluate each possible move means finding them all and then closely examining each one for every possible counter move. If there were 50 possible moves for each of which your opponent could make 50 counter moves, then the total number of possibilities is 2,500. Examining this many possibilities is a difficult enough task, but when you start thinking one, two, or three moves ahead, it becomes impossible. It is so impossible that even a huge electronic computer cannot play a game of draughts in this fashion.

No one ever uses this ideal way of game-playing except perhaps for noughts and crosses. Other techniques have to be used.

Comments on the second day:
1. The first type of competitive situation is one in which the possible moves are so limited and so well known that success depends on psychological manoeuvres.
2. The second type of competitive situation is one in which the possible moves are so numerous that success depends on understanding the complexity of the situation better than the opponent does.

3. The perfect way to play a game is to find out all the possible moves and to evaluate them according to the possible consequences.
4. The above task becomes impossible if the number of moves is large or if it is necessary to think several moves ahead.
5. There are other techniques for choosing a move.

Problem 3

On the following page are nine game settings. Decide which of the nine settings are similar to the first one, *A*, as rapidly as possible. It is suggested that you tackle this problem when you have reached page 139.

In the last section it was noted that the ideal way to play the game was at best very tedious and at worst impossible. In contrast there is another method which is as simple as the first was complicated. This almost effortless method is the method of experience. At each turn you use experience as a guide to what move you ought to make. You imitate what has happened before without making any attempt to find all the possible moves, let alone assess them.

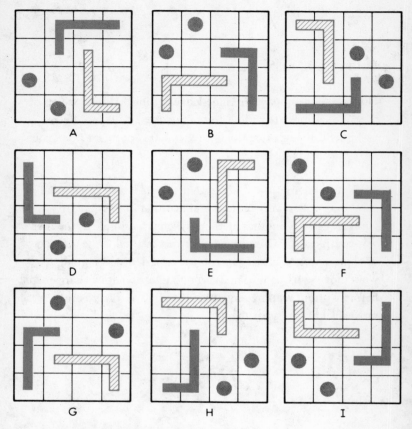

Game Setting for Problem 3

The easiest way to win games with this method is to lose them. Each time you lose you note two things. You note the move which loses you the game and you note the move with which

your opponent wins the game. If your memory is good enough
and you play a sufficient number of times, you will surely
build up a repertoire of two types of moves or, rather, two
types of positions: winning positions and losing positions.
Once you have acquired such a repertoire, all you need do
thereafter is to avoid one type of position and seek out the
other. As your experience increases, you may be bold enough
to learn moves that lead to winning moves. In this way you
may start to think one move ahead.

It may seem to you that this method is as tiresome as the other,
since it means playing a large number of games before you can
really get started. It may not seem much fun to lose game after
game until all your friends tire of playing you just when you
are becoming expert. The method may seem most ineffective
until you have acquired a vast amount of experience.

In practice the games you would play in order to lose would
be very short ones, for you would not have to deliberate over
your moves. Nor would it be difficult to play a sufficient
number of such games, since there are plenty of people
around who always enjoy an opportunity to win a game. In
order to use the method effectively you would not need to
experience all possible moves. For any given setting you would
simply see if there was any winning move to be made or losing
move to be avoided. If there were neither, you would be free
to make any move. Should the move turn out to be a losing
one after all, your experience would be enriched by it.

Solution to Problem 3

The game settings functionally identical to the first one, *A*, are settings *B*, *E*, and *I*. These settings involve simple changes of the positions of the board or mirror-image transformations. In all the other settings the relationship of the pieces has been altered by a change in position of one of the pieces.

The same move would do for any of the functionally identical settings. The great difficulty in actual play is to recognize a familiar situation when it is presented as a mirror image or in a different orientation. Nor is it only in games that we fail to recognize things we know. In order to use the method of experience with any success at all, it is essential to be able to recognize immediately a familiar arrangement for which a move is already known.

Since there are four sides to the board, an arrangement may occur in four different orientations – facing north, south, east, or west. With each of these orientations a mirror-image transformation might occur. That gives eight apparently different settings when the board is looked at from any one side as it is during play. Each of these eight variations may occur either to you or to your opponent. Thus you have to be ready to recognize a familiar setting in all its sixteen different

guises before you can hope to use the experience method
effectively.

It is not supposed that you had any difficulty in solving
Problem 3 correctly, but it would have been interesting to have
timed how long it took you.

All those who think that this business of recognition is easy
with so simple a game will, of course, have noticed that the
arrangement used in the previous problem (Problem 2) was
none other than a mirror image of the starting position of the
game turned on its side to confuse you. If you did recognize
this, you might have been consoled in that tedious problem by
the thought that it would be most useful to assess all the
possible moves from the starting position in order to avoid
first-move blunders. There is nothing more ignominious than
being beaten in the first move.

Comments on the third day:
1. It is possible to play the game by the method of simple
   experience. This method is as effortless as the complete
   assessment method is tedious.
2. The experience method means that you imitate past
   situations, you use moves with which you are familiar.
3. There are two types of moves to be used. Winning moves
   are sought out and losing moves avoided. If there is no
   appropriate move in either category, any move may be made.

4. The quickest way to acquire experience is to play a number of games with the intention of losing. With each game you add a winning position and a losing position to your repertoire of familiar positions.
5. In order to use the experience method effectively, it is necessary to recognize settings even if they are in a different orientation, are transposed into a mirror image, or occur to your opponent.

PROBLEM 4

Below are shown a game setting and three possible moves.
Select the best move.

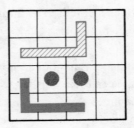

Game Setting

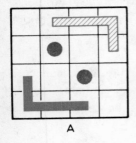

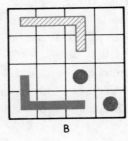

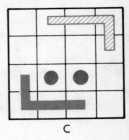

A   B   C

Possible Moves

You may be disappointed in a course which has so far suggested two rather impractical methods of playing the L game. On the other hand, you may feel superior in the knowledge that your own method of play would be better than either of the two methods.

The third method falls somewhere between the two extremes of the previous methods, and yet in a way it makes feasible both of the previous methods. The third method is the method of strategic principles.

The method of full assessment of all possible moves and their consequences was seen to be hopelessly lengthy. Such a method would be much easier if the moves were dealt with in classes or categories. For instance, the number of moves to be considered would be reduced by a factor of thirteen if L-piece moves alone were considered. If there were some general principle for accepting or rejecting at once certain L positions, all the thirteen positions associated with a particular L position could be disposed of with one decision.

By dealing with entire classes of moves in the above manner, it becomes practical to make a full assessment of all possible moves. Strategic principles might be the following:

Seek out corner L positions.
Avoid symmetrical arrangements of the pieces.
Always keep a neutral piece in contact with your L piece.

Seek to nestle your L piece in the angle of the opponent's L piece. These are not necessarily correct. They are only examples of the sort of principles you will form for yourself as you play the game.

But where do the strategic principles come from? A few people may arrive at such principles by logical examination of the nature of the game, a few others may learn them from friends, but most often they are learned through personal experience.

The experience method of play was impractical because until you had played a large number of games your chances of winning would be slight. You may, as suggested previously, have consoled yourself with the thought that every defeat added to your experience, but winning is more fun. Is it possible to gain enough experience without having to play so many games? Paradoxically this is possible – through the use of strategic principles. If you succeed in drawing universal principles from a limited amount of experience, such principles will do instead of further experience since they would hold true in any future game.

Thus we see that by using strategic principles either the experience method or the full assessment method is employed satisfactorily. More simply, the strategic principle method could be said to make possible a full assessment of moves on the basis of principles derived from experience and used to assess whole classes of moves.

Solution to Problem 4

Below are given the counter moves for the moves offered in the problem.

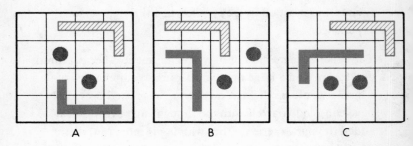

A   B   C

It may be seen that only move *B* is fatal. Both other moves are safe. This outcome may surprise those who had already formed the strategic principle that corner positions were dangerous and to be avoided. On the other hand, all those who worked on the principle that corner L positions were desirable would automatically have made the right choice through avoiding the only non-corner position offered.

The strategic principle policy (sometimes called the heuristic approach in learned circles) is undoubtedly the most practical way to play the game, and it is the way computers are taught to play complicated games. The policy is, however, no better than the value of the principles used. If you formulate a doubtful principle, your use of it may lead to defeat. Principles derived by logic from examination of the game are usually safe, but those derived from experience may well be incorrect if they are based on insufficient experience. Nevertheless, it is probably better to use an incorrect principle and then modify it as required than to be wary of drawing up principles in case they prove wrong.

Even correct principles have some disadvantage because of their general nature. Thus it may be useful to consider all symmetrical settings as undesirable, and yet one of them may be useful. Application of the general principle would mean that the exceptional position would never be tried. As you get more familiar with the principles, you may find that you can handle the exceptions as well.

Comments on the fourth day:
1. The most useful method of playing games is the strategic principle method.
2. Use of strategic principles makes it possible to carry out full assessments of possible moves by considering entire classes of moves.
3. Strategic principles may be derived from logical analysis of the game, from experienced players, or from direct personal experience.

4. Valid strategic principles greatly reduce the amount of playing experience that is necessary in order to play a good game.

5. Incorrect strategic principles lead to defeat.

6. It is probably better to use incorrect principles and improve them as required than to use none at all.

7. On account of their generality the principles may obscure useful exceptions.

8. With sufficient experience exceptions can be handled without interfering with the general principles.

PROBLEM 5

This problem is in two parts:

A. Diagram *A*, below, shows a game setting. It is assumed that you have already moved your L piece and are about to move a neutral piece. Choose the best possible move for a neutral piece.

B. Diagram *B* shows another game setting. Again choose the best move for a neutral piece.

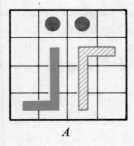

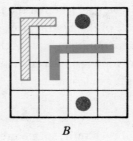

A   *B*

It is natural to assume that the L piece is more important than the neutral piece. For one thing, moving the neutral pieces is only optional and, for another, the L pieces belong to the players and the neutral pieces do not. Furthermore, it is more difficult to find a position for the L piece, and the game is lost when no new position can be found. The L piece is also bigger. In spite of all this, the neutral pieces may be more important. Whether an L position is fatal or not may depend on the placement of a neutral piece. Winning a game may depend on the proper use of these pieces.

You will have to decide for yourself the values and respective roles of the two types of pieces. You may feel that the L piece is a liability since a new position must be found for it and that the neutral piece is really the attacking piece. On the other hand you may feel that the L piece is all-important and that the role of the neutral piece is to support the L strategies. In any situation that requires the handling of two different things, the way interest is divided between each of them can greatly affect the outcome.

The rules of the L game do not require a neutral piece to be moved each turn; such a move is optional. If you are unable to decide to which position to move a neutral piece, you may prefer not to move one at all. This seems the easy way out, for it apparently relieves you of the responsibility for making a decision. In fact this lack of a decision is a very real decision. Leaving pieces as they are does not mean that you have not committed yourself to a decision. On the contrary, it means that you have positively decided that the present position of the neutral pieces is the best possible one. The absence of a decision to do something is, in practical terms, the same as a definite decision to do nothing, even though it may feel very different.

The opposite extreme is reached by those people who feel that since it is possible to move a neutral piece, such a piece must always be moved in order to get the maximal advantage. I have seen people destroy a winning position on account of this greediness.

Solution to Problem 5A

Below is shown the best possible position for the neutral piece. In choosing this position you would have won the game, for the solid L piece cannot now be moved to a new position. If you were really observant, you would have noticed that a similar winning position was used against you before (counter move *B* of Problem 1, page 128). This is the sort of observation that could make the difference between an adequate player and a good one.

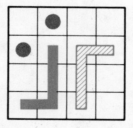

The important point about this solution is that through a correct choice of move it is possible to win the game. There are very many other safe moves for the neutral pieces, but this is the only attacking one. If you had been content simply to find a safe position, you would have missed the chance of winning.

The entire attitude of attacking and defending is a matter of temperament. You may be one of those people who are always eager to find an attacking position and if you cannot do so are somewhat careless about securing a good defensive position. On the other hand, you may be so unsure of your skill that you first try to secure a safe position and only look for an attacking position afterwards, and in a perfunctory manner.

Solution to Problem 5B

Below is shown the best position for the neutral pieces arising from setting *B* on page 149. In contrast to Problem 5A, the choice of position is here an entirely defensive one. There is no question of an attacking position. On the contrary, the position shown is the only safe one (or so it seems to me), and all others are dangerous.

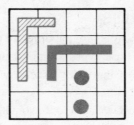

The attacking and defending attitudes are not alternative policies. Some settings may require one attitude and some the other. All settings require a *consideration* of both. In choosing a move we usually go through a hierarchy of aims. The first aim is to find a winning position. If this is not possible, the next aim is to avoid a losing position.

With increasing experience this hierarchy of aims can be extended. As both players become familiar with winning and losing positions, success comes to depend on being able to think one move ahead. Thus it is not enough merely to choose a winning position; you ought to be able to choose a position that will lead to a winning position on the next turn. Next you start planning two moves ahead and so on. This means that, after you have found that an outright winning position is impossible, the next aim in the hierarchy is not to find a safe move, but to find a move that will lead to a winning move.

Comments on the fifth day:
1. When a game involves moving different types of pieces, the roles ascribed to these types will affect the outcome.
2. An apparently less significant piece may actually turn out to be more important.
3. Inability to make a decision to do something is the same as a definite decision to do nothing – even though it may feel different.

4. An attacking attitude or a defending one may determine the choice of move. With a defending attitude a possible winning move may be overlooked.

5. Some situations call for an attacking policy, others only allow a defending one.

6. In choosing a move it is usual to go through a hierarchy of intentions or aims. These may be as follows: choose a winning move; choose a move that will lead to a winning move; avoid a losing move.

7. The player who can think the most moves ahead wins.

8. It is not necessary to make all available moves on each occasion. Such greediness may have a disadvantage.

Reading about a game and solving relatively simple problems is no substitute for playing the game. In actual play there is a continually changing situation, there is the necessity to make decision after decision, and there is also the possibility of learning from experience. Playing a game is also a practical rather than an academic business. It is not possible to take ages to work out the best move. Practical and simplifying short cuts have to be developed for choosing moves.

The L game is amusing because it is so extremely simple and yet offers an opportunity to exercise and develop policies that could be useful in much more complicated situations.

The L game is a miniature game, and in some ways games themselves are miniature life situations. In the isolated purity of a game there is an opportunity to practise skills of learning and strategy that may have wider applications.

The comments offered were not meant to be an exhaustive or authoritative treatise on how to play games. As in the other courses, the comments are bait for your own ideas, either through gentle suggestion or through fury at the banality of those offered.

In these courses each reader has been his own laboratory. The purpose of the book has been to shift attention from the problems themselves to the way the mind tackles them. The problems are not tests, but practical opportunities to be fascinated by the processes of thinking. Why a problem appears to be difficult may be much more interesting than the solution itself.

The ideas that you develop about the processes of thinking are at least as valid as those suggested. From such ideas may arise a realization that the mind does not behave in the ideal logical way. Some of the problems appear very simple once they have been solved, and yet they may have been difficult to solve. What is it that prevents a problem with a simple solution from being solved with ease? Is it just a lack of logical efficiency? Sometimes it seems that the very efficiency of logic may lead one off in the wrong direction.

In practice thinking is a rather messy business; it is not just a matter of following the rules of logic. The approach to a problem is usually more important than the efficiency with which that approach is followed up. The choice of approach may be determined by habit, by an attitude of mind, or even by emotion.

Some people may have had difficulty with the problems

because they were unwilling to let go of the obvious and so became trapped by it. With others the self-imposed necessity to proceed carefully from stage to stage may have made impossible a solution that required a more imaginative step at some point. The very words used to describe a problem to oneself may have affected the ease with which it could be solved, for even a description may impose a rigidity that limits the approaches to the solution. These and many other points may have been noted.

The way new ideas come about or fail to come about may have made all the difference. It soon becomes obvious that you cannot dig a hole in a different place by digging the same hole deeper. A gradual distinction emerges between two fundamentally different sorts of thinking. With 'vertical' thinking one tries to dig the same hole deeper and proceeds rigidly along the path with the highest probability. With 'lateral' thinking one proceeds imaginatively along a variety of low-probability paths in the hope of generating a new and better approach to the problem. The difference between vertical and lateral thinking is a fundamental one.

It is these attitudes of mind and these strategies of thinking that are important. They are dictated by the nature of the brain and not by the importance of the problems that are being tackled. From a realization of the personal and general deficiencies of the mind may grow a better skill in thinking. The study of difficulty in thinking may serve a more useful purpose than an attempt to capture the nature of intelligence.